A POST HILL PRESS BOOK

The Socialists:
Do As We Say, Not As We Do
© 2019 by Post Hill Press
All Rights Reserved

ISBN:978-1-64293-348-2

Post Hill Press
New York • Nashville
posthillpress.com

Published in the United States of America

American Toxic

POISON ALEX